United States
Department of
Agriculture

Forest Service

**Southern
Research Station**

Resource Bulletin
SRS–151

Alabama's Timber Industry—
An Assessment of Timber Product
Output and Use, 2007

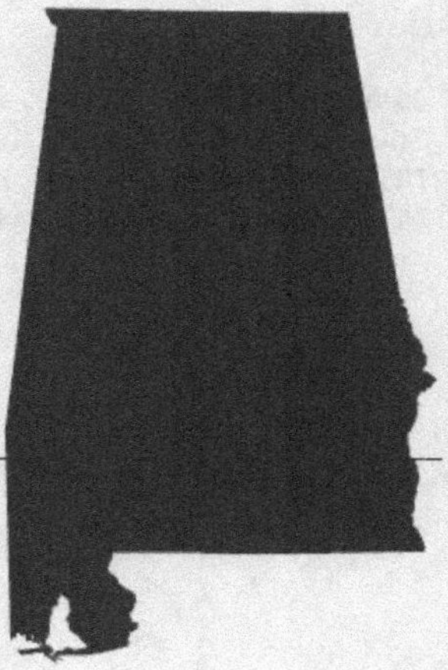

James R. Schiller
and Brian Hendricks

The Authors:

James R. Schiller, Forester, U.S. Forest Service, Southern Research Station, Knoxville, TN 37919; and **Brian Hendricks**, FIA Coordinator, Alabama Forestry Commission, Montgomery, AL 36104.

June 2009

Southern Research Station
200 W.T. Weaver Blvd.
Asheville, NC 28804

Foreword

This report contains the findings of a 2007 canvass of all primary wood-using plants in Alabama, and presents changes in product output and residue use since 2005. It complements the Forest Inventory and Analysis (FIA) periodic inventory of volume and removals from the State's timberland. The canvass was conducted to determine the amount and source of wood receipts and annual timber product drain, by county, in 2007 and to determine interstate and cross-regional movement of industrial roundwood. Only primary wood-using mills were canvassed. Primary mills are those that process roundwood in log or bolt form or as chipped roundwood. Examples of industrial roundwood products are saw logs, pulpwood, veneer logs, poles, and logs used for composite board products. Mills producing products from residues generated at primary and secondary processors were not canvassed. Trees chipped in the woods were included in the estimate of timber drain only if they were delivered to a primary domestic manufacturer.

A 100-percent canvass of all wood processors in Alabama was conducted in 2008 to obtain information for 2007. In addition, roundwood from out-of-State mills known to be using logs or bolts harvested from Alabama timberland was incorporated into Alabama production estimates. Each mill was canvassed by mail or through personal contact at plant locations. Telephone contacts followed mailed questionnaire responses when additional information or clarification of a response was necessary. In the event of a nonresponse,

data collected in previous surveys were updated using current data collected for mills of similar size, product type, and location. Surveys for all timber products other than pulpwood began in 1961, and are currently conducted every 2 years.

Pulpwood production data were taken from an annual canvass of all southern pulpmills. Medium density fiberboard, insulating board, and hardboard plants were included in this survey.

Acknowledgments

The authors thank Gene Quick and Allen Varner for review and comments; Carolyn Steppleton and Michael Howell for their tireless efforts in processing and accuracy of the data; Helen Beresford for timber product output database maintenance and support; Anne Jenkins, Janet Griffin, Sharon Johnson, and Charlene Walker for tables, graphs, and statistical checking; and the Southern Research Station (SRS) Technical Publications Team for editorial review, styling, and publication of this report.

The SRS gratefully acknowledges the cooperation and assistance provided by the Alabama Forestry Commission in collecting mill data. Appreciation is also extended to forest industry and mill managers for providing timber products information.

Timber Product Output Database Retrieval System

The Forest Inventory and Analysis (FIA) Research Work Unit of the USDA Forest Service developed the Timber Product Output (TPO) Database Retrieval System to help customers answer questions about timber harvesting and use in the Southern Region. This system acts as an interface to a standard set of consistently coded TPO data for each State and county in the region and Nation. This regional and national set of TPO data consists of 11 variables that describe for each county the roundwood products harvested, logging residues left in the woods, other timber removals (i.e. land clearing and reserved timber removals), and wood and bark residues generated by the county's primary wood-using mills. The system is available through the FIA Web site: http://srsfia2.fs.fed.us/.

The database is well documented and easy to use. The retrieval system allows the user to select the TPO variables of interest and generate a standard set of timber products, removals, and mill residue tables for the specified resource area, State, or region. The system has been logically divided into two sections to assist the user in making specific data requests. In section 1, the user is asked to define the resource area, and section 2 generates tables for the specified area. In each section, the user is asked to supply specific options that will serve to customize the database retrieval.

There are four options available for defining the geographic area of interest. Each option provides an increasing level of detail. The region, subregion, State, or county defines an area. The user selects the option that best suits the level of detail required. Users who select county as an option should be aware that some counties have been combined due to data sensitivity. These combined counties are identified with asterisks in the output tables.

The TPO contacts are listed for each region to provide additional explanation or clarification.

Tony Johnson
Southern Research Station
USDA Forest Service
4700 Old Kingston Pike
Knoxville, TN 37919
tjohnson09@fs.fed.us
865-862-2042

Helen Beresford
Southern Research Station
USDA Forest Service
4700 Old Kingston Pike
Knoxville, TN 37919
hberesford@fs.fed.us
865-862-2091

James Bentley
Southern Research Station
USDA Forest Service
4700 Old Kingston Pike
Knoxville, TN 37919
jbentley@fs.fed.us
865-862-2056

Carolyn Steppleton
Southern Research Station
USDA Forest Service
200 W.T. Weaver Blvd.
Asheville, NC 28804
csteppleton@fs.fed.us
828-257-4848

Contents

[a] All tables in this report are available in Microsoft® Excel workbook files. Upon request, these files will be supplied in the format the customer requests.

The use of trade or firm names in this publication is for reader information and does not imply endorsement by the U.S. Department of Agriculture of any product or service.

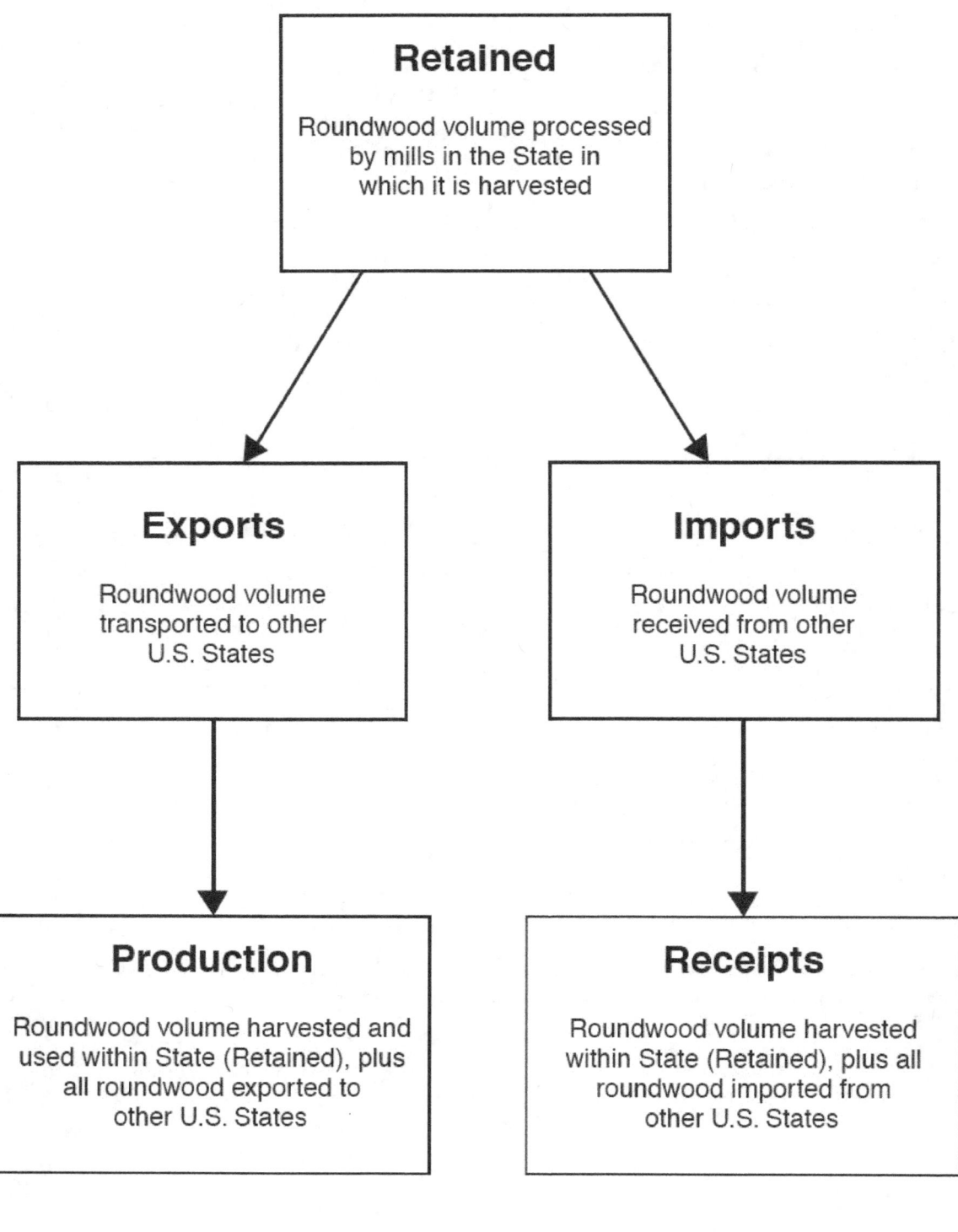

Figure 1—Movement of roundwood exports and imports within the United States.

Alabama's Timber Industry—An Assessment of Timber Product Output and Use, 2007

James R. Schiller and Brian Hendricks

Output of Industrial Timber Products

Note: Certain terms used in this report—retained, export, import, production, and receipts—have specialized meanings and relationships unique to the Forest Inventory and Analysis Units across the country that deal with timber product output (TPO) (fig. 1).

All Products

- TPO from roundwood was down 41 million cubic feet, or 4 percent, to 1.10 billion cubic feet, while output of utilized plant byproducts was down 53 million cubic feet to 379 million cubic feet.

- Output of softwood roundwood products decreased 6 percent to 828 million cubic feet, while output of hardwood roundwood products increased 4 percent to 274 million cubic feet (fig. 2).

- Pulpwood and saw logs were the principal roundwood products in 2007. Combined output of these products totaled 987 million cubic feet and accounted for 90 percent of Alabama's total roundwood output (fig. 3).

- Total receipts at Alabama mills, which included roundwood harvested and retained in the State as well as roundwood imported from other States, decreased 6 percent to 1.12 billion cubic feet. The number of primary roundwood-using plants in Alabama totaled 144 in 2007, a loss of 1 mill since 2005 (fig. 4).

- Across all products, 84 percent of roundwood harvested was retained for processing at Alabama mills. Exports of roundwood to other States amounted to 171 million cubic feet, while imports of roundwood amounted to 185 million cubic feet making the State a net importer of roundwood. Tables A.8 to A.11 show exports to and imports from other States by individual product type.

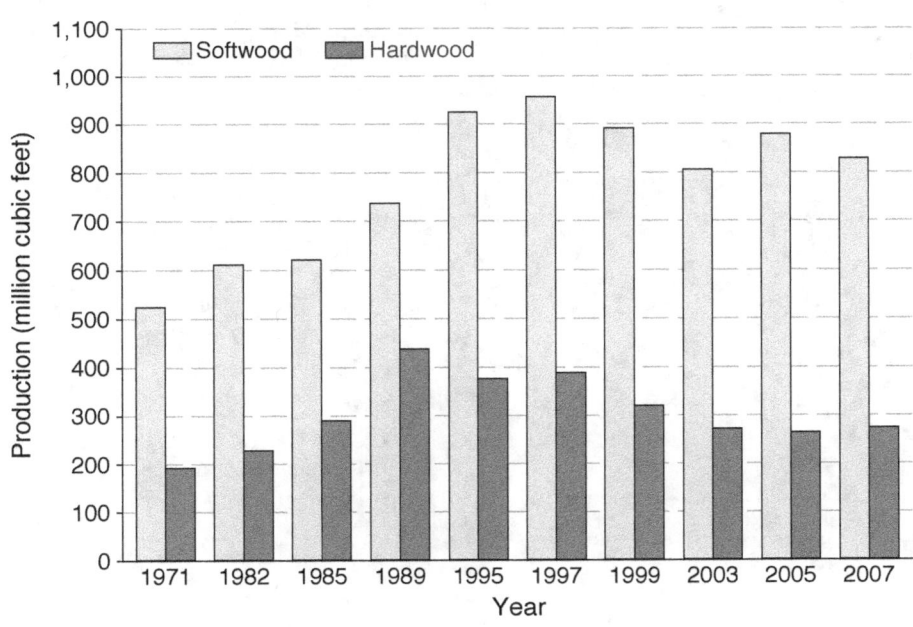

Figure 2—Roundwood production for all products by species group and year, (see page 8 for references for individual years), Alabama.

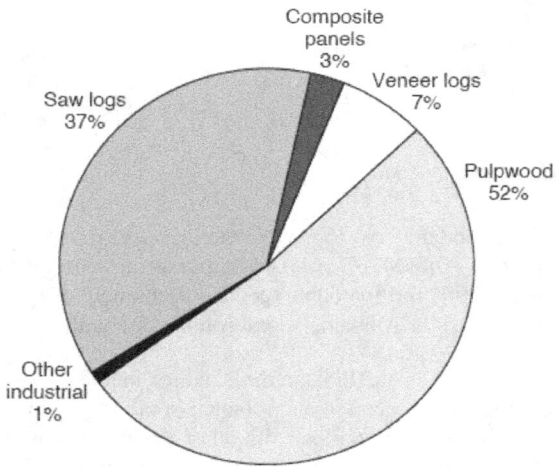

Total 1.1 billion cubic feet

Figure 3—Roundwood production by type of product, Alabama, 2007.

Pulpwood

- Total pulpwood production, including chipped round-wood, increased 11 million cubic feet to 574 million cubic feet (7.94 million cords) and accounted for 52 percent of the State's total roundwood TPO. Softwood output increased 1 percent to 375 million cubic feet; hardwood output increased 5 percent to 199 million cubic feet (fig. 5).

- Fourteen pulpmill facilities were operating and receiving roundwood in Alabama in 2007, the same as in 2005. Total pulpwood receipts for these mills increased 12 million cubic feet to 604 million cubic feet, accounting for 54 percent of total receipts for all mills.

- Eighty-three percent of roundwood cut for pulpwood was retained for processing at Alabama pulpmills. Round-wood pulpwood accounted for 56 percent of total known exports and 68 percent of total imports. Roundwood pulpwood imports amounted to 126 million cubic feet, 30 million cubic feet more than was exported.

Saw Logs

- Saw logs accounted for 37 percent of the State's total roundwood products. Output of softwood saw logs decreased 5 percent to 355 million cubic feet (1.97 billion board feet, International ¼-inch rule), while that of hard-wood saw logs rose 8 percent to 58 million cubic feet (346 million board feet, International ¼-inch rule) (fig. 6).

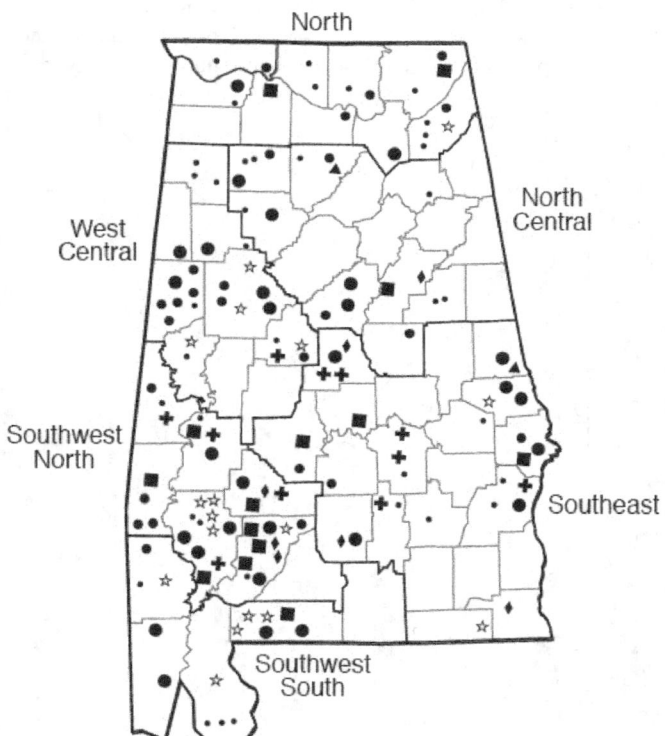

Primary wood-using mills

- • Sawmill (0–5 mmbf)
- ● Sawmill (5–20 mmbf)
- ⬤ Sawmill (>20 mmbf)
- ▲ Composite panel
- ✚ Veneer
- ■ Pulpmill
- ◆ Plywood
- ☆ Other

Figure 4—Primary wood-using mills by region, Alabama, 2007.

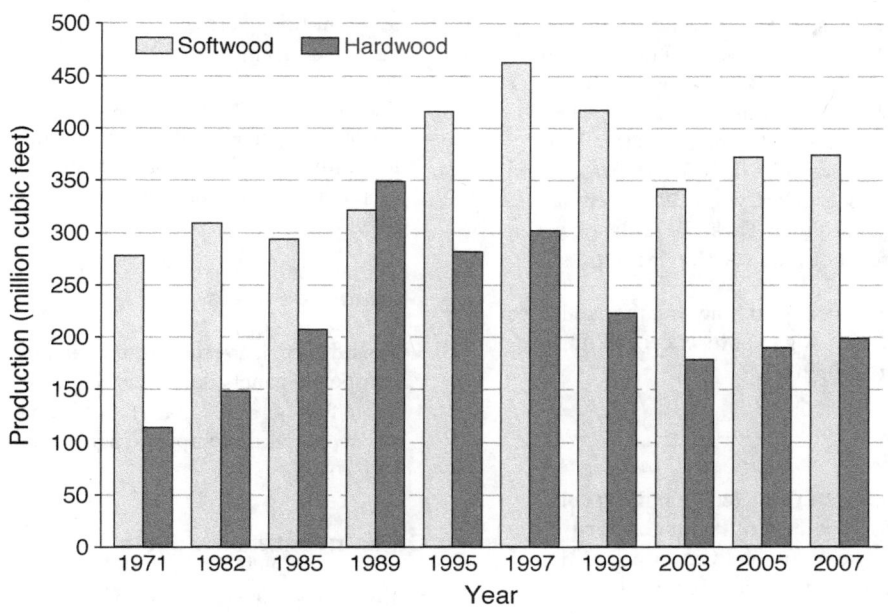

Figure 5—Roundwood pulpwood production by species group and year (see page 8 for references for individual years), Alabama.

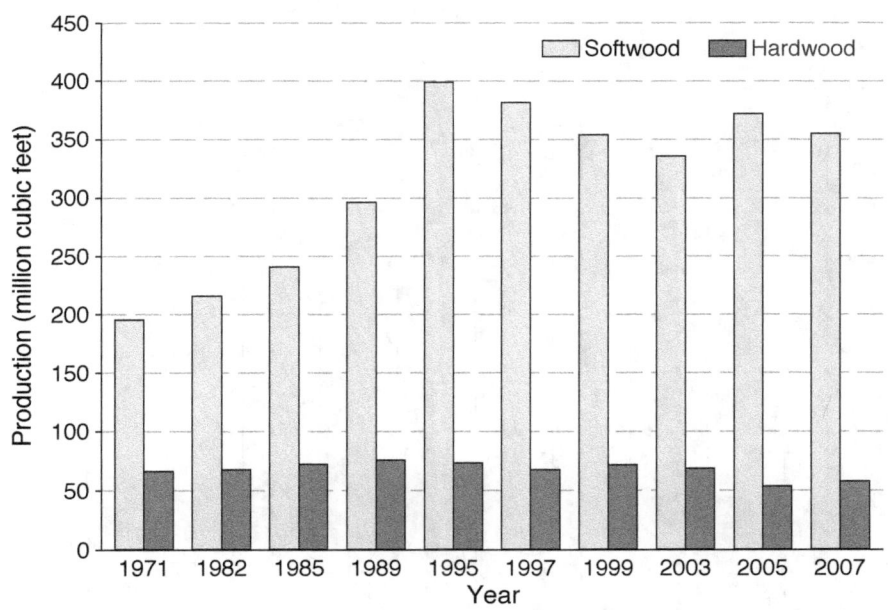

Figure 6—Roundwood saw-log production by species group and year (see page 8 for references for individual years), Alabama.

- In 2007, Alabama had 93 sawmills, the same number as 2005. Total saw-log receipts decreased 50 million cubic feet to 394 million cubic feet. Softwood saw-log receipts were down 14 percent to 334 million cubic feet, while those of hardwoods increased 11 percent to 60 million cubic feet. Of the operating mills in 2007, 17 percent had receipts of <1 million board feet, while 32 percent had receipts >10 million board feet. These 30 mills, however, accounted for 92 percent of total saw-log receipts.

- Alabama retained 84 percent of its saw-log production for in-State manufacture; saw-log exports exceeded imports by 19 million cubic feet in 2007.

Veneer Logs

- Output of veneer logs in 2007 totaled 75 million cubic feet and accounted for 7 percent of the State's total roundwood TPO volume. Softwood veneer production decreased 19 percent to 60 million cubic feet (351 million board feet, International ¼-inch rule); output of hardwood veneer logs declined 20 percent to 15 million cubic feet (93 million board feet, International ¼-inch rule) (fig. 7).

- Eighteen veneer mills were operating in Alabama in 2007. Total receipts of veneer logs decreased 17 percent

to 72 million cubic feet. Softwood veneer receipts decreased 10 million cubic feet to 58 million cubic feet.

- Alabama retained 89 percent of its veneer-log production for processing at in-State veneer mills. Imports amounted to 5 million cubic feet, and exports totaled 8 million cubic feet, making the State a net exporter of roundwood veneer logs.

Composite Panels

- Roundwood harvested from Alabama's forests for composite panels decreased 35 percent to 29 million cubic feet (412,929 cords). Softwood output accounted for nearly all of composite panel production in Alabama (fig. 8).

Other Industrial Products

- Roundwood harvested for other industrial uses, such as poles, posts, mulch, firewood, and all other industrial products, decreased 36 percent to 10 million cubic feet. Other industrial product volume accounted for 1 percent of the State's total TPO volume. Softwood output accounted for nearly all of the industrial product volume.

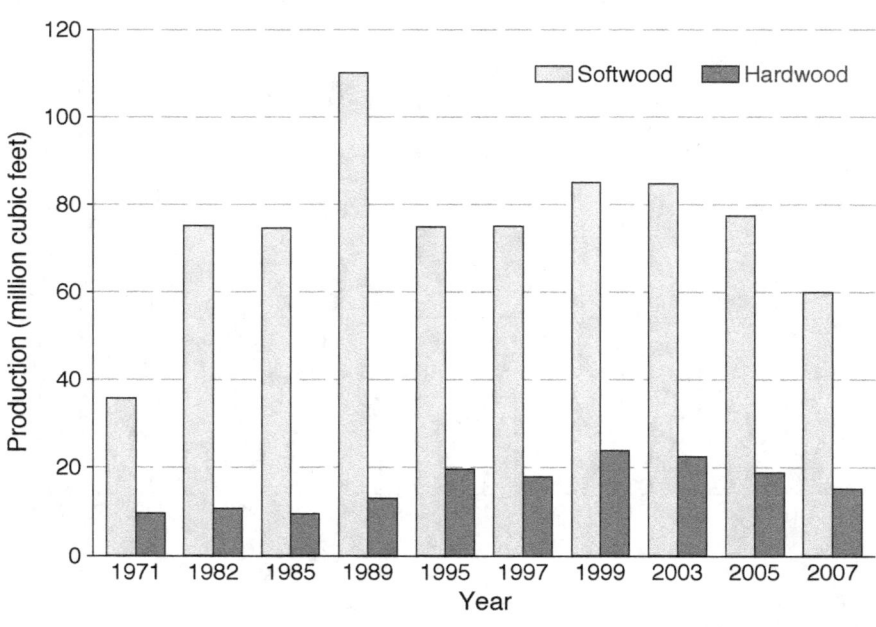

Figure 7—Roundwood veneer-log production by species group and year (see page 8 for references for individual years), Alabama.

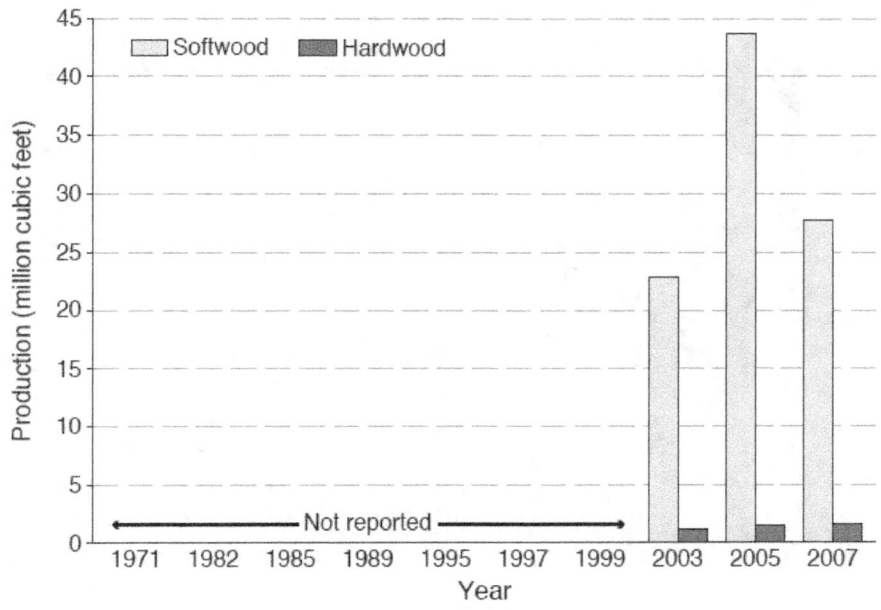

Figure 8—Roundwood production for composite panels by species group and year (see page 8 for references for individual years), Alabama.

Plant Byproducts

- In 2007, processing of primary products in Alabama mills generated 379 million cubic feet of wood and bark residues. Bark residues from all primary products were 134 million cubic feet, while coarse volume totaled 135 million cubic feet. Sawdust and shavings made up 29 percent of total residues, or 110 million cubic feet (fig. 9).

- The processing of saw logs generated 234 million cubic feet of mill residues, accounting for 62 percent of the total residues produced (fig. 10).

- Virtually all of the wood and bark residues were used for a product; <1 percent were not used, while 56 percent of the residues were used for industrial fuel (fig. 11). Almost 120 million cubic feet, or 89 percent, of the coarse residues were used to manufacture fiber products. Most of the bark was used for industrial fuel or other miscellaneous products, while 72 percent of the sawdust and shavings were used for industrial fuel.

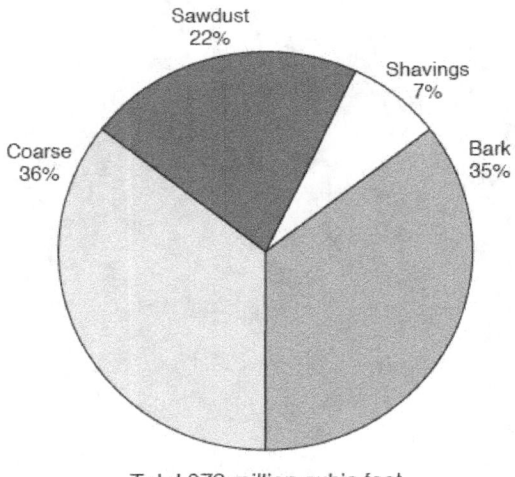

Total 379 million cubic feet

Figure 9—Primary mill residue by residue type, Alabama, 2007.

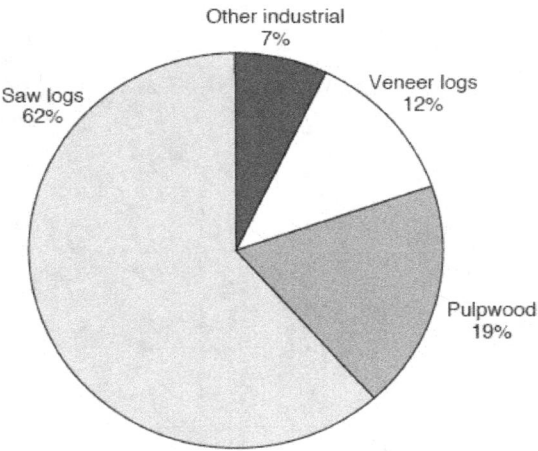

Total 379 million cubic feet

Figure 10—Primary mill residue produced by roundwood type, Alabama, 2007.

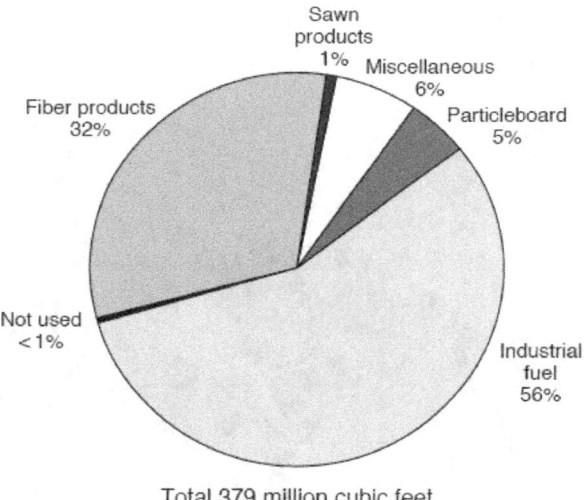

Total 379 million cubic feet

Figure 11—Disposal of residue by product, Alabama, 2007.

County Data

- Table A.14 shows softwood and hardwood product output by county and individual product type. All 67 counties in Alabama had softwood and hardwood output. Eight counties (Choctaw, Clarke, Conecuh, Marengo, Monroe, Sumter, Washington, and Wilcox) had combined softwood and hardwood product output of > 30 million cubic feet

each. These eight counties total product output amounted to > 331 million cubic feet and accounted for 30 percent of the State's total product output.

Total Roundwood Output

Using the most recent inventory data for Alabama, product output by source, ownership, and detailed species group was estimated.

Source

- In addition to the 1.10 billion cubic feet of roundwood output for industrial roundwood products, an estimated 20 million cubic feet was harvested for domestic fuel-wood, bringing Alabama's total roundwood output to 1.12 billion cubic feet.

- Ninety-one percent of total roundwood output was considered growing-stock volume (sawtimber and poletimber) from timberland sources. Other sources (such as saplings; stumps, tops, and limbs of trees on timberland; and trees on nonforest land) contributed an estimated 97 million cubic feet, or 9 percent of total roundwood output (fig. 12).

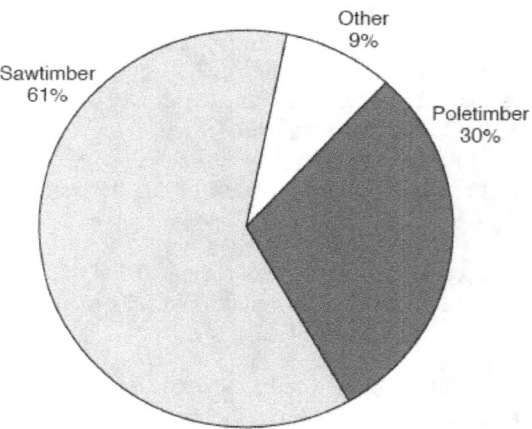

Total 1.1 billion cubic feet

Figure 12—Roundwood output by source, Alabama, 2007.

Ownership

- An estimated 830 million cubic feet, or 74 percent, of the total roundwood output came from nonindustrial private forest lands. Forest industry lands contributed 256 million cubic feet, or 23 percent of the output. Public lands made up the remaining 3 percent, or 36 million cubic feet (fig. 13).

Species

- The loblolly and shortleaf pine group provided more volume than any other softwood species group, accounting for 86 percent of the total softwood output (fig. 14). The longleaf and slash pine type accounted for 11 percent of the softwood output. The red oak and white oak groups combined accounted for 124 million cubic feet, or 43 percent of total hardwood output (fig. 15).

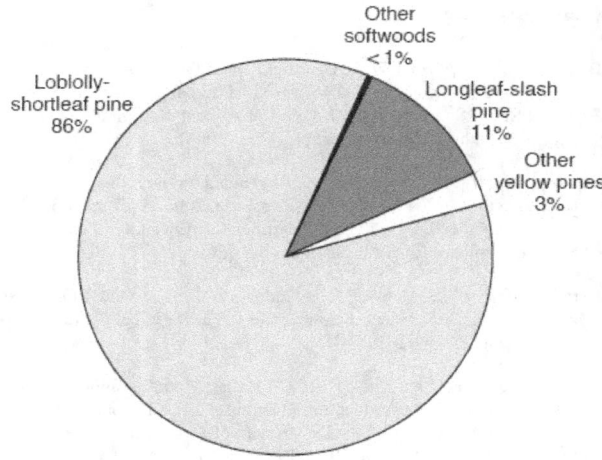

Total 831 million cubic feet

Figure 14—Roundwood output by softwood species group, Alabama, 2007.

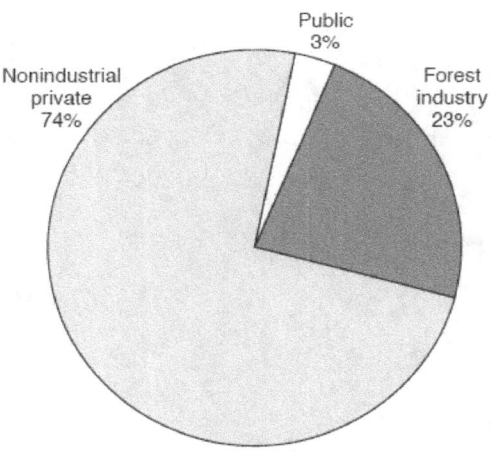

Total 1.1 billion cubic feet

Figure 13—Roundwood output by ownership, Alabama, 2007.

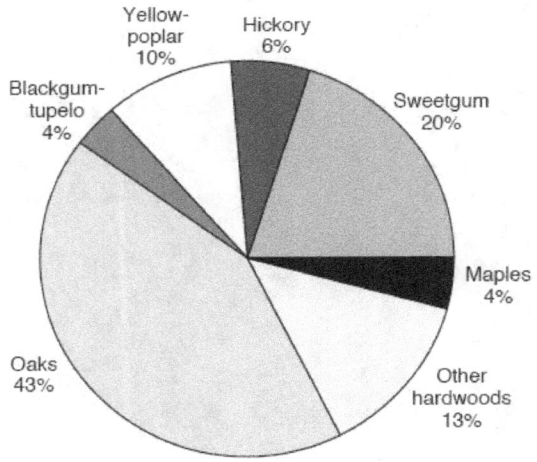

Total 291 million cubic feet

Figure 15—Roundwood output by hardwood species group, Alabama, 2007.

References

Bentley, J.W.; Cartwright W.E.; Hendricks, B. 2008. Alabama's timber industry—an assessment of timber product output and use, 2005. Resour. Bull. SRS–128. Asheville, NC: U.S. Department of Agriculture Forest Service, Southern Research Station. 32 p. [2005].

Bentley, J.W.; Cartwright W.E. 2006. Alabama's timber industry—an assessment of timber product output and use, 2003. Resour. Bull. SRS–107. Asheville, NC: U.S. Department of Agriculture Forest Service, Southern Research Station. 45 p. [2003].

Bertelson, D.F. 1972. Alabama forest industries. Resour. Bull. SO–36. New Orleans: U.S. Department of Agriculture Forest Service, Southern Forest Experiment Station. 29 p. [1971].

Howell, M.; Gober, J.R.; Nix, J.S. 2002. Alabama's timber industry—an assessment of timber product output and use, 1999. Resour. Bull. SRS–75. Asheville, NC: U.S. Department of Agriculture Forest Service, Southern Research Station. 39 p. [1999].

Howell, M.; Gober, J.R.; Nix, J.S. 1999. Alabama's timber industry—an assessment of timber product output and use, 1997. Resour. Bull. SRS–45. Asheville, NC: U.S. Department of Agriculture Forest Service, Southern Research Station. 36 p. [1997].

Johnson, T.G.; Gober, J.R.; Nix, J.S. 1998. Alabama's timber industry—an assessment of timber product output and use, 1995. Resour. Bull. SRS–27. Asheville, NC: U.S. Department of Agriculture Forest Service, Southern Research Station. 28 p. [1995].

Little, E.L., Jr. 1979. Checklist of United States trees (native and naturalized). Agric. Handb. 541. Washington, DC: U.S. Department of Agriculture. 375 p.

Sternitzke, H.S. 1963. Alabama forest industries. Resour. Bull. SO–3. New Orleans: U.S. Department of Agriculture Forest Service, Southern Forest Experiment Station. 32 p. [1962].

Tennessee Valley Authority. Timber product removals by county and species group. Division of Land and Economic Resources, Forest Resources Development Program. 4 p. Unpublished data. On file with: Southern Research Station, U.S. Department of Agriculture Forest Service, Forest Inventory and Analysis Research Work Unit, 4700 Old Kingston Pike, Knoxville, TN 37919. [1982, 1985, 1989].

Glossary

Board foot. A unit of measure applied to lumber that is 1-foot long, 1-foot wide, and 1-inch thick (or its equivalent) and also associated with roundwood as to its potential yield of such products.

Byproducts. Primary wood products, e.g., pulp chips, animal bedding, and fuelwood, recycled from mill residues.

Composite panels. Roundwood products manufactured into chips, wafers, strands, flakes, shavings, or sawdust and then reconstituted into a variety of panel and engineered lumber products.

Consumption. The quantity of a commodity, such as pulpwood, utilized by a particular mill or group of mills.

Domestic fuelwood. The volume of roundwood harvested to produce heat for residential settings.

Drain. The volume of roundwood removed from any geographic area where timber is grown.

Exports. The volume of domestic roundwood utilized by mills outside the State where timber was cut.

Fiber products. Byproducts used in the manufacture of pulp, paper, paperboard, and composite products, such as chipboard.

Growing-stock removals. The growing-stock volume removed from poletimber and sawtimber trees in the timberland inventory. (Note: Includes volume removed for roundwood products, logging residues, and other removals.)

Growing-stock trees. Living trees of commercial species classified as sawtimber, poletimber, saplings, and seedlings. Growing-stock trees must contain at least one 12-foot or two 8-foot logs in the saw-log portion, currently or potentially (if too small to qualify). The log(s) must meet dimension and merchantability standards and have, currently or potentially, one-third of the gross board-foot volume in sound wood.

Growing-stock volume. The cubic-foot volume of sound wood in growing-stock trees at least 5.0 inches d.b.h. from a 1-foot stump to a minimum 4.0-inch top d.o.b. of the central stem.

Hardwoods. Dicotyledonous trees, usually broadleaf and deciduous.

Soft hardwoods. Hardwood species with an average specific gravity of 0.50 or less, such as gums, yellow-poplar, cottonwoods, red maple, basswoods, and willows.

Hard hardwoods. Hardwood species with an average specific gravity >0.50, such as oaks, hard maples, hickories, and beech.

Imports. The volume of domestic roundwood delivered to a mill or group of mills in a specific State but harvested outside that State.

Industrial fuelwood. A roundwood product, with or without bark, used to generate energy at a manufacturing facility such as a wood-using mill.

Industrial roundwood products. Any primary use of the main stem of a tree, such as saw logs, pulpwood, veneer logs, intended to be processed into primary wood products such as lumber, wood pulp, sheathing, at primary wood-using mills.

International ¼-inch rule. A log rule or formula for estimating the board-foot volume of logs, allowing ½-inch of taper for each 4-foot length. The rule appears in a number of forms that allow for kerf. In the form used by FIA, a ¼-inch of kerf is assumed. This rule is used as the U.S. Forest Service standard log rule in the Eastern United States.

Log. A primary forest product harvested in long, primarily 8-, 12-, and 16-foot lengths.

Logging residues. The unused merchantable portion of growing-stock trees cut or destroyed during logging operations.

Merchantable portion. That portion of live trees 5.0 inches d.b.h. and larger between a 1-foot stump and a minimum 4.0-inch top d.o.b. on the central stem. That portion of primary forks from the point of occurrence to a minimum 4.0-inch top d.o.b. is included.

Merchantable volume. Solid-wood volume in the merchantable portion of live trees.

Noncommercial species. Tree species of typically small size, poor form, or inferior quality that normally do not develop into trees suitable for industrial wood products.

Nonforest land. Land that has never supported forests and land formerly forested where timber production is precluded by development for other uses.

Nongrowing-stock sources. The net volume removed from the nongrowing-stock portions of poletimber and sawtimber trees (stumps, tops, limbs, cull sections of central stem) and from any portion of a rough, rotten, sapling, dead, or nonforest tree.

Other forest land. Forest land other than timberland and productive reserved forest land. It includes available and reserved forest land that is incapable of producing annually 20 cubic feet per acre of industrial wood under natural conditions because of adverse site conditions such as sterile soils, dry climate, poor drainage, high elevation, steepness, or rockiness.

Other products. A miscellaneous category of roundwood products, e.g., cooperage, excelsior, shingles, and mill residue byproducts (charcoal, bedding, mulch, etc.).

Other removals. The growing-stock volume of trees removed from the inventory by cultural operations such as timber stand improvement, land clearing, and other changes in land use, resulting in the removal of the trees from timberland.

Other sources. (See: Nongrowing-stock sources.)

Ownership. The property owned by one ownership unit, including all parcels of land in the United States.

National forest land. Federal land that has been legally designated as national forests or purchase units, and other land under the administration of the Forest Service, including experimental areas and Bankhead-Jones Title III land.

Forest industry land. Land owned by companies or individuals operating primary wood-using plants.

Nonindustrial private forest (NIPF) land. Privately owned land excluding forest industry land.

    Corporate. Owned by corporations, including incorporated farm ownerships.

    Individual. All lands owned by individuals, including farm operators.

Other public. An ownership class that includes all public lands except national forests.

    Miscellaneous Federal land. Federal land other than national forests.

    State, county, and municipal land. Land owned by States, counties, and local public agencies or municipalities, or land leased to these governmental units for 50 years or more.

Plant residues. Wood material generated in the production of timber products at primary manufacturing plants.

Coarse residues. Material, such as slabs, edgings, trim, veneer cores and ends, which is suitable for chipping.

Fine residues. Material, such as sawdust, shavings, and veneer residue, which is not suitable for chipping.

Plant byproducts. Residues (coarse or fine) used in the further manufacture of industrial products for consumer use, or as fuel.

Unused plant residues. Residues (coarse or fine) that are not used for any product, including fuel.

Poletimber-size trees. Softwoods 5.0 to 8.9 inches d.b.h. and hardwoods 5.0 to 10.9 inches d.b.h.

Posts, poles, and pilings. Roundwood products milled (cut or peeled) into standard sizes (lengths and circumferences) to be put in the ground to provide vertical and lateral support in buildings, foundations, utility lines, and fences. May also include nonindustrial (unmilled) products.

Primary wood-using plants. Industries that convert roundwood products (saw logs, veneer logs, pulpwood, etc.) into primary wood products, such as lumber, veneer or sheathing, wood pulp.

Production. The total volume of known roundwood harvested from land within a State, regardless of where it is consumed. Production is the sum of timber harvested and used within a State, and all roundwood exported to other States.

Pulpwood. A roundwood product that will be reduced to individual wood fibers by chemical or mechanical means. The fibers are used to make a broad generic group of pulp products that includes paper products, as well as fiberboard, insulating board, and paperboard.

Receipts. The quantity or volume of industrial roundwood received at a mill or by a group of mills in a State, regardless of the geographic source. Volume of roundwood receipts is equal to the volume of roundwood retained in a State plus roundwood imported from other States.

Retained. Roundwood volume harvested from and processed by mills within the same State.

Rotten trees. Live trees of commercial species not containing at least one 12-foot saw log, or two noncontiguous saw logs, each 8 feet or longer, now or prospectively, primarily because of rot or missing sections, and with less than one-third of the gross board-foot tree volume in sound material.

Rough trees. Live trees of commercial species not containing at least one 12-foot saw log, or two noncontiguous saw logs, each 8 feet or longer, now or prospectively, primarily because of roughness, poor form, splits, and cracks, and with less than one-third of the gross board-foot tree volume in sound material; and live trees of noncommercial species.

Roundwood (roundwood logs). Logs, bolts, or other round sections cut from trees for industrial manufacture or consumer uses.

Roundwood chipped. Any timber cut primarily for industrial manufacture, delivered to nonpulpmills, chipped, and then sold to pulpmills for use as fiber. Includes tops, jump sections, whole trees, and pulpwood sticks.

Roundwood product drain. That portion of total drain used for a product.

Roundwood products. Any primary product, such as lumber, veneer, composite panels, poles, pilings, pulp, or fuelwood that is produced from roundwood.

Salvable dead trees. Standing or downed dead trees that were formerly growing stock and considered merchantable. Trees must be at least 5.0 inches d.b.h. to qualify.

Saplings. Live trees 1.0 to 5.0 inches d.b.h.

Saw log. A roundwood product, usually 8 feet in length or longer, processed into a variety of sawn products such as lumber, cants, pallets, railroad ties, and timbers.

Saw-log portion. The part of the bole of sawtimber trees between a 1-foot stump and the saw-log top.

Saw-log top. The point on the bole of sawtimber trees above which a conventional saw log cannot be produced. The minimum saw-log top is 7.0 inches d.o.b. for softwoods and 9.0 inches d.o.b. for hardwoods for FIA standards.

Sawtimber-size trees. Softwoods 9.0 inches d.b.h. and larger and hardwoods 11.0 inches d.b.h. and larger.

Sawtimber volume. Growing-stock volume in the saw-log portion of sawtimber-sized trees in board feet (International ¼-inch rule).

Seedlings. Trees < 1.0 inch d.b.h. and > 1 foot tall for hardwoods, > 6 inches tall for softwoods, and > 0.5 inch in diameter at ground level for longleaf pine.

Select red oaks. A group of several red oak species composed of cherrybark, Shumard, and northern red oaks. Other red oak species are included in the "other red oaks" group.

Select white oaks. A group of several white oak species composed of white, swamp chestnut, swamp white, chinkapin, Durand, and bur oaks. Other white oak species are included in the "other white oaks" group.

Softwoods. Coniferous trees, usually evergreen, having leaves that are needles or scale like.

Standard cord. A unit of measure applied to roundwood, usually bolts or split wood. It is a stack of wood 4 feet high, 4 feet wide, and 8 feet long encompassing 128 cubic feet of wood, bark, and air space. This usually translates to approximately 75.0 to 81.0 cubic feet of solid wood for pulpwood, because pulpwood is more uniform.

Standard unit. A unit measure applied to roundwood timber products. Board feet (International ¼-inch rule) is the standard unit used for saw logs and veneer; cords are used for pulpwood, composite panel, and fuelwood; hundred pieces for poles; thousand pieces for posts; and thousand cubic feet for all other miscellaneous forest products.

Timberland. Forest land capable of producing 20 cubic feet of industrial wood per acre per year and not withdrawn from timber utilization.

Timber product output. The total volume of roundwood products from all sources plus the volume of byproducts recovered from mill residues (equals roundwood product drain).

Timber products. Roundwood products and byproducts.

Timber removals. The total volume of trees removed from the timberland inventory by harvesting, cultural operations such as stand improvement, land clearing, or changes in land use. (Note: Includes roundwood products, logging residues, and other removals.)

Tree. Woody plants having one erect perennial stem or trunk at least 3 inches d.b.h., a more or less definitely formed crown of foliage, and a height of at least 13 feet (at maturity).

Upper-stem portion. The part of the main stem of sawtimber trees above the saw-log top and the minimum top diameter of 4.0 inches outside bark, or to the point where the main stem breaks into limbs.

Utilization studies. Studies conducted on active logging operations to develop factors for merchantable portions of trees left in the woods (logging residues), logging damage, and utilization of the unmerchantable portion of growing-stock trees and nongrowing-stock trees.

Veneer log. A roundwood product either rotary cut, sliced, stamped, or sawn into a variety of veneer products such as plywood, finished panels, veneer sheets, or sheathing.

Weight. A unit of measure for mill residues, expressed as oven-dry tons (2,000 oven-dry pounds).

Conversion Factors[a]

Saw logs	
Softwood	0.18018 cubic foot = 1 board foot
	5.55 board feet = 1 cubic foot
Hardwood	0.16807 cubic foot = 1 board foot
	5.95 board feet = 1 cubic foot
Veneer logs	
Softwood	0.17094 cubic foot = 1 board foot
	5.85 board feet = 1 cubic foot
Hardwood	0.16260 cubic foot = 1 board foot
	6.15 board feet = 1 cubic foot
Pulpwood[b]	
Softwood	71 cubic feet per cord
Hardwood	75 cubic feet per cord

[a] Conversion factors vary with stem size (d.b.h.) and species. The factors shown are for trees of average diameters removed in Alabama during the most recent survey period.

[b] Cubic feet of solid wood per cord.

Species List[a]

Common name	Scientific name[b]	Common name	Scientific name[b]
Softwoods		**Hardwoods (continued)**	
Atlantic white-cedar	*Chamaecyparis thyoides* (L.) B.S.P.	American holly	*Ilex opaca* Ait.
Southern redcedar	*Juniperus silicicola* (Small) Bailey	Black walnut	*Juglans nigra* L.
Eastern redcedar	*J. virginiana* L.	Sweetgum	*Liquidambar styraciflua* L.
Shortleaf pine	*Pinus echinata* Mill.	Yellow-poplar	*Liriodendron tulipifera* L.
Slash pine	*P. elliottii* Engelm.	Osage-orange	*Maclura pomifera* (Raf.) Schneid.
Spruce pine	*P. glabra* Walt.	Cucumbertree	*Magnolia acuminata* L.
Longleaf pine	*P. palustris* Mill.	Southern magnolia	*M. grandiflora* L.
Pond pine	*P. serotina* Michx.	Bigleaf magnolia	*M. macrophylla* Michx.
Eastern white pine	*P. strobus* L.	Sweetbay	*M. virginiana* L.
Loblolly pine	*P. taeda* L.	Apple	*Malus* spp. Mill.
Virginia pine	*P. virginiana* Mill.	Chinaberry	*Melia azedarach* L.
Baldcypress	*Taxodium distichum* (L.) Rich.	White mulberry	*Morus alba* L.
Pondcypress	*T. distichum* var. *nutans* (Aiton) Sweet	Red mulberry	*M. rubra* L.
Eastern hemlock	*Tsuga canadensis* (L.) Carr.	Water tupelo	*Nyssa aquatica* L.
		Blackgum	*N. sylvatica* Marsh.
Hardwoods		Swamp tupelo	*N. sylvatica* var. *biflora* (Walt.) Sarg.
Florida maple	*Acer barbatum* Michx.	Eastern hophornbeam	*Ostrya virginiana* (Mill.) K. Koch
Boxelder	*A. negundo* L.	Sourwood	*Oxydendrum arboreum* (L.) DC.
Red maple	*A. rubrum* L.	Redbay	*Persea borbonia* (L.) Spreng.
Silver maple	*A. saccharinum* L.	American sycamore	*Platanus occidentalis* L.
Sugar maple	*A. saccharum* Marsh.	Cottonwood	*Populus* spp. L.
Buckeye	*Aesculus* spp. L.	Black cherry	*Prunus serotina* Ehrh.
Ohio buckeye	*A. glabra* Willd.	White oak	*Quercus alba* L.
Ailanthus	*Ailanthus altissima* (Mill.) Swingle	Scarlet oak	*Q. coccinea* Muenchh.
Tung-oil tree	*Aleurites fordii* Hemsl.	Durand oak	*Q. durandii* Buckl.
Serviceberry	*Amelanchier* spp. Med.	Southern red oak	*Q. falcata* Michx.
River birch	*Betula nigra* L.	Cherrybark oak	*Q. falcata* var. *pagodifolia* Ell.
American hornbeam	*Carpinus caroliniana* Walt.	Bluejack oak	*Q. incana* Bartr.
Hickory	*Carya* spp. Nutt.	Turkey oak	*Q. laevis* Walt.
Water hickory	*C. aquatica* (Michx. f.) Nutt.	Laurel oak	*Q. laurifolia* Michx.
Bitternut hickory	*C. cordiformis* (Wangenh.) K. Koch	Overcup oak	*Q. lyrata* Walt.
Pignut hickory	*C. glabra* (Mill.) Sweet	Swamp chestnut oak	*Q. michauxii* Nutt.
Pecan	*C. illinoensis* (Wangenh.) K. Koch	Chinkapin oak	*Q. muehlenbergii* Engelm.
Shellbark hickory	*C. laciniosa* (Michx. f.) Loud.	Water oak	*Q. nigra* L.
Nutmeg hickory	*C. myristiciformis* (Michx. f.) Nutt.	Nuttall oak	*Q. nuttallii* Palmer
Shagbark hickory	*C. ovata* (Mill.) K. Koch	Pin oak	*Q. palustris* Muenchh.
Black hickory	*C. texana* Buckl.	Willow oak	*Q. phellos* L.
Mockernut hickory	*C. tomentosa* (Poir.) Nutt.	Chestnut oak	*Q. prinus* L.
Allegheny chinkapin	*Castanea pumila* Mill.	Northern red oak	*Q. rubra* L.
Chinkapin	*Castanopsis* (D. Don) Spach	Shumard oak	*Q. shumardii* Buckl.
Catalpa	*Catalpa* spp. Scop.	Post oak	*Q. stellata* Wangenh.
Sugarberry	*Celtis laevigata* Willd.	Black oak	*Q. velutina* Lam.
Hackberry	*C. occidentalis* L.	Live oak	*Q. virginiana* Mill.
Eastern redbud	*Cercis canadensis* L.	Black locust	*Robinia pseudoacacia* L.
Flowering dogwood	*Cornus florida* L.	Willow	*Salix* spp. L.
Hawthorn	*Crataegus* spp. L.	Sassafras	*Sassafras albidum* (Nutt.) Nees
Common persimmon	*Diospyros virginiana* L.	American basswood	*Tilia americana* L.
American beech	*Fagus grandifolia* Ehrh.	White basswood	*T. heterophylla* Vent.
White ash	*Fraxinus americana* L.	Winged elm	*Ulmus alata* Michx.
Pumpkin ash	*F. profunda* (Bush) Bush	American elm	*U. americana* L.
Blue ash	*F. quadrangulata* Michx.	Cedar elm	*U. crassifolia* Nutt.
Waterlocust	*Gleditsia aquatica* Marsh.	Slippery elm	*U. rubra* Muhl.
Honeylocust	*G. triacanthos* L.	September elm	*U. serotina* Sarg.
Kentucky coffeetree	*Gymnocladus dioicus* (L.) K. Koch	Rock elm	*U. thomasii* Sarg.

[a] Scientific and common names of tree species ≥ 1.0 inch d.b.h. occurring in the FIA sample.
[b] Little (1979).

13

Appendix

Index of Tables

Table A.1—Output of industrial products by product and species group, Alabama, 2005 and 2007

Product and species group	Year		Change	Change
	2005	2007		
	- - - - - - thousand cubic feet - - - - - -			percent
Saw logs				
Softwood	371,660	354,977	-16,683	-4.5
Hardwood	53,636	58,030	4,394	8.2
Total	425,296	413,007	-12,289	-2.9
Veneer logs				
Softwood	74,444	60,069	-14,375	-19.3
Hardwood	18,824	15,100	-3,724	-19.8
Total	93,268	75,169	-18,099	-19.4
Pulpwood[a]				
Softwood	372,736	374,966	2,230	0.6
Hardwood	190,046	199,131	9,085	4.8
Total	562,782	574,097	11,315	2.0
Composite panels				
Softwood	43,760	27,777	-15,983	-36.5
Hardwood	1,509	1,610	101	6.7
Total	45,269	29,387	-15,882	-35.1
Other industrial				
Softwood	16,108	10,306	-5,802	-36.0
Hardwood	60	100	40	66.7
Total	16,168	10,406	-5,762	-35.6
All industrial				
Softwood	878,708	828,095	-50,613	-5.8
Hardwood	264,075	273,971	9,896	3.7
Total	1,142,783	1,102,066	-40,717	-3.6

[a] Includes roundwood delivered to nonpulpmills, then chipped and sold to pulpmills (9,401,000 cubic feet in 2005 and 4,084,000 cubic feet in 2007).

Table A.2—Roundwood receipts by product and species group, Alabama, 2005 and 2007

Product and species group	Year		Change	Change
	2005	2007		
	- - - - - - thousand cubic feet - - - - - -			percent
Saw logs				
Softwood	389,422	333,878	-55,544	-14.3
Hardwood	54,176	60,099	5,923	10.9
Total	443,598	393,977	-49,621	-11.2
Veneer logs				
Softwood	68,084	57,619	-10,465	-15.4
Hardwood	18,231	14,399	-3,832	-21.0
Total	86,315	72,018	-14,297	-16.6
Pulpwood[a]				
Softwood	331,407	339,975	8,568	2.6
Hardwood	260,607	264,147	3,540	1.4
Total	592,014	604,122	12,108	2.0
Other industrial				
Softwood	59,816	44,471	-15,345	-25.7
Hardwood	1,338	1,448	110	8.2
Total	61,154	45,919	-15,235	-24.9
Total output				
Softwood	848,729	775,943	-72,786	-8.6
Hardwood	334,352	340,093	5,741	1.7
Total	1,183,081	1,116,036	-67,045	-5.7

[a] Includes roundwood delivered to nonpulpmills, then chipped and sold to pulpmills (10,659,000 cubic feet in 2005 and 4,477,000 cubic feet in 2007).

Table A.3—Number of primary wood-using plants by type of mill, Alabama, 1962 to 2007

Type of mill	Year									
	1962	1971	1982	1985	1995	1997	1999	2003	2005	2007
	number									
Sawmills	555	323	239	250	148	145	121	118	93	93
Veneer mills	34	32	28	28	23	26	23	23	19	18
Pulpmills	9	15	16	16	16	16	15	14	14	14
Composite panel mills	0	0	0	0	1	1	1	2	2	2
Other mills	47	36	35	47	23	24	21	21	17	17
All plants	645	406	318	341	211	212	181	178	145	144

Table A.4—Roundwood receipts by sawmill size, Alabama, 2005 and 2007

Sawmill size class[a]	2005			2007		
	Mills	Volume		Mills	Volume	
mmbf	*number*	*mbf*	*percent*	*number*	*mbf*	*percent*
< 1.0	15	4,557	0	16	5,130	0
1.0–4.99	19	43,422	2	22	64,613	3
5.0–9.99	18	136,244	5	25	107,722	5
10.0–49.99	21	472,251	19	14	656,061	30
> 50	20	1,829,705	74	16	1,379,376	62
Total	93	2,486,179	100	93	2,212,902	100

[a] Based on volume received as opposed to actual capacity.

Table A.5—Roundwood receipts by species and type of mill, Alabama, 2007

| | | | Type of mill | | | |
| | | | Veneer mills | | | |
Species	All mills	Sawmills	Pine plywood	Other veneer	Pulpmills[a]	Other mills
			thousand cubic feet			
Softwood						
Yellow pine	433,275	331,755	57,553	60	NA	43,907
White pine	5	5	0	0	NA	0
Cedar	1,164	1,019	0	0	NA	145
Cypress	1,370	945	6	0	NA	419
Other softwood	154	154	0	0	NA	0
Unclassified	339,975	0	0	0	339,975	0
Total softwoods	775,943	333,878	57,559	60	339,975	44,471
Hardwood						
Blackgum-tupelo	1,452	913	69	294	NA	176
Soft maple	695	430	73	14	NA	178
Sweetgum	8,343	5,266	317	2,228	NA	532
Yellow-poplar	11,219	5,920	834	3,936	NA	529
Other soft hardwood	2,332	2,249	69	14	NA	0
Hickory	2,415	1,895	1	506	NA	13
Red oak	29,546	26,090	53	3,388	NA	15
White oak	16,942	15,151	3	1,783	NA	5
Other hard hardwood	3,002	2,185	0	817	NA	0
Unclassified	264,147	0	0	0	264,147	0
Total hardwoods	340,093	60,099	1,419	12,980	264,147	1,448
All species	1,116,036	393,977	58,978	13,040	604,122	45,919

NA = not applicable.

[a] Only collected by softwood and hardwood and includes roundwood chipped.

Table A.6—Industrial roundwood movement by year and species group, Alabama, 2005 and 2007

Year	Production	Exported to other States	Retained	Imported from other States	Receipts
			thousand cubic feet		
		Softwood			
2005	878,708	151,691	727,017	121,712	848,729
2007	828,095	157,057	671,038	104,905	775,943
		Hardwood			
2005	264,075	20,114	243,961	90,391	334,352
2007	273,971	14,337	259,634	80,459	340,093
		All species			
2005	1,142,783	171,805	970,978	212,103	1,183,081
2007	1,102,066	171,394	930,672	185,364	1,116,036

Table A.7—Industrial roundwood movement by product and species group, Alabama, 2007

Product and species group	Production	Exported to other States	Retained	Imported from other States	Receipts
			thousand cubic feet		
Saw logs					
Softwood	354,977	59,336	295,641	38,237	333,878
Hardwood	58,030	6,523	51,507	8,592	60,099
Total	413,007	65,859	347,148	46,829	393,977
Veneer logs					
Softwood	60,069	7,844	52,225	5,394	57,619
Hardwood	15,100	787	14,313	86	14,399
Total	75,169	8,631	66,538	5,480	72,018
Pulpwood[a]					
Softwood	374,966	88,934	286,032	53,943	339,975
Hardwood	199,131	6,765	192,366	71,781	264,147
Total	574,097	95,699	478,398	125,724	604,122
Other industrial					
Softwood	38,083	943	37,140	7,331	44,471
Hardwood	1,710	262	1,448	0	1,448
Total	39,793	1,205	38,588	7,331	45,919
All products					
Softwood	828,095	157,057	671,038	104,905	775,943
Hardwood	273,971	14,337	259,634	80,459	340,093
Total	1,102,066	171,394	930,672	185,364	1,116,036

[a] Includes roundwood delivered to nonpulpmills, then chipped and sold to pulpmills.

Table A.8—Saw-log volume by destination, source, and species group, Alabama, 2007

Destination and source	All species	Species group	
		Softwood	Hardwood
	thousand cubic feet		
Alabama (retained)	347,148	295,641	51,507
Exports to			
Florida	24,787	24,781	6
Georgia	14,019	13,123	896
Mississippi	22,820	21,365	1,455
Missouri	45	0	45
Tennessee	4,188	67	4,121
Total	65,859	59,336	6,523
Imports from			
California	251	0	251
Florida	5,601	5,601	0
Georgia	15,804	15,559	245
Kentucky	74	74	0
Mississippi	19,604	12,899	6,705
Tennessee	5,495	4,104	1,391
Total	46,829	38,237	8,592

Table A.9—Veneer volume by destination, source, and species group, Alabama, 2007

Destination and source	All species	Species group	
		Softwood	Hardwood
	thousand cubic feet		
Alabama (retained)	66,538	52,225	14,313
Exports to			
Georgia	1,446	668	778
Mississippi	7,184	7,176	8
South Carolina	1	0	1
Total	8,631	7,844	787
Imports from			
Florida	930	926	4
Georgia	3,623	3,541	82
Mississippi	927	927	0
Total	5,480	5,394	86

Table A.10—Pulpwood volume by destination, source, and species group, Alabama, 2007[a]

Destination and source	All species	Species group	
		Softwood	Hardwood
	thousand cubic feet		
Alabama (retained)	478,398	286,032	192,366
Exports to			
Arkansas	3	0	3
Florida	16,706	16,694	12
Georgia	37,819	34,068	3,751
Kentucky	1,541	0	1,541
Louisiana	50	3	47
Mississippi	26,358	26,357	1
North Carolina	142	0	142
Tennessee	13,078	11,811	1,267
Texas	1	0	1
Virginia	1	1	0
Total	95,699	88,934	6,765
Imports from			
Florida	7,578	6,560	1,018
Georgia	45,775	33,011	12,764
Mississippi	40,325	8,821	31,504
Tennessee	32,046	5,551	26,495
Total	125,724	53,943	71,781

[a] Includes roundwood delivered to nonpulpmills, then chipped and sold to pulpmills.

Table A.11—Other industrial volume by destination, source, and species group, Alabama, 2007[a]

Destination and source	All species	Species group	
		Softwood	Hardwood
	thousand cubic feet		
Alabama (retained)	38,588	37,140	1,448
Exports to			
Georgia	55	0	55
Mississippi	437	437	0
Tennessee	713	506	207
Total	1,205	943	262
Imports from			
Florida	827	827	0
Georgia	6,390	6,390	0
Kentucky	42	42	0
Mississippi	72	72	0
Total	7,331	7,331	0

[a] Includes composite panels, poles, posts, mulch, firewood, log homes, charcoal, and all other industrial products.

Table A.12—Primary mill residue volume by roundwood type, species group, and residue type, Alabama, 2007

Roundwood type and species group	All types	Residue type			
		Bark	Coarse	Sawdust	Shavings
		thousand cubic feet			
Saw logs					
Softwood	199,778	30,079	92,021	50,055	27,623
Hardwood	33,857	6,866	13,969	12,608	414
Total	233,635	36,945	105,990	62,663	28,037
Veneer logs					
Softwood	38,038	5,466	17,675	14,897	0
Hardwood	9,638	1,697	3,555	4,386	0
Total	47,676	7,163	21,230	19,283	0
Pulpwood					
Softwood	37,265	37,265	0	0	0
Hardwood	33,214	33,214	0	0	0
Total	70,479	70,479	0	0	0
Other industrial[a]					
Softwood	26,920	19,436	7,415	69	0
Hardwood	384	365	14	5	0
Total	27,304	19,801	7,429	74	0
Total					
Softwood	302,001	92,246	117,111	65,021	27,623
Hardwood	77,093	42,142	17,538	16,999	414
Total	379,094	134,388	134,649	82,020	28,037

[a] Includes poles, pilings, posts, and other industrial products.

Table A.13—Disposal of residue at primary wood-using plants by product, species group, and type of residue, Alabama, 2005 and 2007

Product and species group	All types		Bark		Coarse		Sawdust		Shavings	
	2005	2007	2005	2007	2005	2007	2005	2007	2005	2007
	thousand cubic feet									
Fiber products										
Softwood	129,251	104,125	0	0	129,005	104,125	227	0	19	0
Hardwood	14,169	15,404	0	0	14,169	15,404	0	0	0	0
Total	143,420	119,529	0	0	143,174	119,529	227	0	19	0
Particleboard										
Softwood	21,271	17,956	0	0	0	0	6,073	4,742	15,198	13,214
Hardwood	24	536	0	0	0	0	0	536	24	0
Total	21,295	18,492	0	0	0	0	6,073	5,278	15,222	13,214
Sawn products										
Softwood	2,975	2,925	0	0	2,975	2,925	0	0	0	0
Hardwood	266	52	0	0	266	52	0	0	0	0
Total	3,241	2,977	0	0	3,241	2,977	0	0	0	0
Industrial fuel										
Softwood	171,067	155,021	89,063	82,726	11,446	9,158	60,646	54,367	9,912	8,770
Hardwood	58,834	58,017	40,184	40,482	1,931	1,704	16,400	15,511	319	320
Total	229,901	213,038	129,247	123,208	13,377	10,862	77,046	69,878	10,231	9,090
Miscellaneous										
Softwood	32,019	21,956	13,289	9,517	1,451	893	9,160	5,907	8,119	5,639
Hardwood	1,723	2,809	1,141	1,474	40	315	517	926	25	94
Total	33,742	24,765	14,430	10,991	1,491	1,208	9,677	6,833	8,144	5,733
Not used										
Softwood	122	18	27	3	75	10	20	5	0	0
Hardwood	65	275	41	186	20	63	4	26	0	0
Total	187	293	68	189	95	73	24	31	0	0
All products										
Softwood	356,705	302,001	102,379	92,246	144,952	117,111	76,126	65,021	33,248	27,623
Hardwood	75,081	77,093	41,366	42,142	16,426	17,538	16,921	16,999	368	414
Total	431,786	379,094	143,745	134,388	161,378	134,649	93,047	82,020	33,616	28,037

Table A.14—Roundwood timber product output by county, product, and species group, Alabama, 2007

County	All products Soft-wood	All products Hard-wood	Saw logs Soft-wood	Saw logs Hard-wood	Veneer logs Soft-wood	Veneer logs Hard-wood	Pulpwood[a] Soft-wood	Pulpwood[a] Hard-wood	Composite panel Soft-wood	Composite panel Hard-wood	Other industrial Soft-wood	Other industrial Hard-wood
						thousand cubic feet						
Autauga	6,397	3,015	2,259	253	411	94	3,727	2,668	0	0	0	0
Baldwin	24,582	2,088	11,211	13	264	58	12,118	2,017	0	0	989	0
Barbour	24,803	4,670	13,675	143	328	209	10,792	4,318	0	0	8	0
Bibb	11,688	8,310	7,036	2,417	536	375	3,581	5,504	153	14	382	0
Blount	4,703	2,790	1,672	262	341	0	237	2,233	2,453	295	0	0
Bullock	10,064	2,106	809	90	706	149	8,549	1,867	0	0	0	0
Butler	21,664	3,307	8,505	221	2,100	357	11,059	2,729	0	0	0	0
Calhoun	4,740	1,173	816	443	1,022	5	2,749	711	153	14	0	0
Chambers	11,000	2,349	4,273	488	1,053	256	2,098	1,605	3,576	0	0	0
Cherokee	9,604	2,559	2,567	425	511	10	6,312	2,110	153	14	61	0
Chilton	8,853	3,795	4,500	1,411	679	527	3,590	1,857	0	0	84	0
Choctaw	28,363	12,560	10,430	2,828	2,354	407	15,187	9,325	0	0	392	0
Clarke	53,617	18,946	25,142	1,509	4,204	2,546	22,987	14,891	0	0	1,284	0
Clay	10,320	3,450	1,848	1,207	1,347	54	7,125	2,189	0	0	0	0
Cleburne	11,674	1,925	3,985	163	1,363	27	6,326	1,735	0	0	0	0
Coffee	5,049	2,314	1,355	93	132	81	3,554	2,140	0	0	8	0
Colbert	3,050	2,238	1,822	871	0	0	1,228	1,367	0	0	0	0
Conecuh	27,644	5,292	7,130	324	4,218	69	15,922	4,899	0	0	374	0
Coosa	14,838	3,451	3,651	1,147	1,557	38	8,980	2,266	536	0	114	0
Covington	26,179	2,985	11,004	21	2,039	69	12,405	2,895	0	0	731	0
Crenshaw	17,140	3,629	8,327	179	1,184	236	7,619	3,214	0	0	10	0
Cullman	6,286	2,499	3,591	405	0	0	242	1,813	2,453	281	0	0
Dale	4,197	2,475	2,317	0	327	45	1,548	2,430	0	0	5	0
Dallas	14,014	7,042	4,428	1,387	608	152	8,702	5,503	0	0	276	0
De Kalb	5,299	4,360	1,944	1,825	341	16	2,440	2,368	559	146	15	5
Elmore	4,719	1,899	1,051	209	633	138	3,035	1,552	0	0	0	0
Escambia	21,433	2,040	11,230	52	1,323	0	7,557	1,988	0	0	1,323	0
Etowah	4,634	2,487	1,453	681	1,022	5	1,086	1,745	1,073	56	0	0
Fayette	9,800	2,621	5,780	1,294	4	208	3,451	1,105	476	14	89	0
Franklin	6,594	2,982	2,359	76	0	0	4,235	2,906	0	0	0	0
Geneva	5,384	312	3,598	0	0	5	1,771	307	0	0	15	0
Greene	15,645	7,805	11,689	3,779	56	577	3,624	3,449	0	0	276	0
Hale	11,988	5,313	4,976	987	211	853	6,784	3,473	0	0	17	0
Henry	7,174	3,050	2,071	2	329	97	4,766	2,951	0	0	8	0
Houston	4,580	464	3,256	6	1	35	1,308	423	0	0	15	0
Jackson	1,370	7,838	740	3,387	0	27	362	4,316	253	103	15	5
Jefferson	4,577	2,175	2,422	1,572	226	174	215	289	1,687	140	27	0
Lamar	14,332	3,223	11,596	1,820	0	0	2,719	1,403	0	0	17	0
Lauderdale	1,897	3,932	923	1,704	0	0	974	2,228	0	0	0	0
Lawrence	1,844	2,140	110	218	0	0	1,581	1,908	153	14	0	0
Lee	15,378	1,120	10,985	19	304	202	3,195	868	894	0	0	31
Limestone	861	1,428	506	843	0	0	202	571	153	14	0	0
Lowndes	10,257	3,288	3,710	221	1,052	774	5,473	2,293	0	0	22	0
Macon	14,297	2,179	5,292	49	407	326	7,168	1,804	1,430	0	0	0

continued

28

Table A.14—Roundwood timber product output by county, product, and species group, Alabama, 2007 (continued)

County	All products Soft-wood	All products Hard-wood	Saw logs Soft-wood	Saw logs Hard-wood	Veneer logs Soft-wood	Veneer logs Hard-wood	Pulpwood[a] Soft-wood	Pulpwood[a] Hard-wood	Composite panel Soft-wood	Composite panel Hard-wood	Other industrial Soft-wood	Other industrial Hard-wood
						thousand cubic feet						
Madison	3,708	2,179	2,567	891	341	5	647	1,269	153	14	0	0
Marengo	26,490	12,661	9,850	1,740	2,311	1,435	14,088	9,486	0	0	241	0
Marion	9,340	3,312	4,317	1,058	0	0	5,023	2,254	0	0	0	0
Marshall	2,305	1,675	1,185	445	170	0	184	1,160	766	70	0	0
Mobile	18,218	5,136	9,001	195	1,357	0	7,385	4,941	0	0	475	0
Monroe	29,952	7,483	10,824	402	6,173	56	12,479	7,025	0	0	476	0
Montgomery	6,924	2,666	2,155	499	860	399	3,909	1,768	0	0	0	0
Morgan	941	1,818	461	350	0	0	327	1,454	153	14	0	0
Perry	8,193	5,873	2,232	2,531	424	11	5,099	3,331	0	0	438	0
Pickens	16,800	7,902	9,884	1,518	146	501	6,669	5,883	0	0	101	0
Pike	7,515	2,700	1,948	422	706	175	4,853	2,103	0	0	8	0
Randolph	8,501	5,122	2,293	400	578	99	4,379	4,568	1,251	0	0	55
Russell	16,413	1,800	9,002	417	0	8	7,054	1,375	357	0	0	0
St. Clair	8,161	3,002	2,629	715	1,193	5	2,192	2,268	2,147	14	0	0
Shelby	7,720	3,366	1,805	1,613	1,406	180	4,272	1,559	153	14	84	0
Sumter	20,982	10,056	11,432	3,073	1,183	1,247	7,965	5,736	0	0	402	0
Talladega	8,143	1,434	1,212	346	1,621	87	5,096	987	153	14	61	0
Tallapoosa	16,711	4,577	4,645	927	1,584	265	6,906	3,381	3,576	0	0	4
Tuscaloosa	13,087	5,928	8,159	3,029	5	367	3,443	2,406	1,073	126	407	0
Walker	6,953	1,251	4,775	846	0	0	924	236	1,227	169	27	0
Washington	27,799	7,872	13,033	769	2,390	87	11,648	7,016	0	0	728	0
Wilcox	33,312	8,450	10,762	280	4,428	972	17,821	7,198	0	0	301	0
Winston	7,395	2,084	2,762	520	0	0	4,020	1,494	613	70	0	0
All counties	828,095	273,971	354,977	58,030	60,069	15,100	374,966	199,131	27,777	1,610	10,306	100

[a] Includes roundwood delivered to nonpulpmills, then chipped and sold to pulpmills (4,084,000 cubic feet in 2007).

Table A.15—Total roundwood output by product, species group, and source of material, Alabama, 2007

| Product and species group | All sources | Total | Growing-stock trees | | Other sources |
			Sawtimber	Poletimber	
			thousand cubic feet		
Saw logs					
Softwood	354,977	343,024	316,268	26,756	11,953
Hardwood	58,030	56,670	53,838	2,833	1,360
Total	413,007	399,694	370,106	29,589	13,313
Veneer logs and bolts					
Softwood	60,069	58,249	55,306	2,943	1,820
Hardwood	15,100	14,839	14,839	0	261
Total	75,169	73,088	70,145	2,943	2,081
Pulpwood					
Softwood	374,966	323,801	120,791	203,010	51,165
Hardwood	199,131	179,749	99,875	79,874	19,382
Total	574,097	503,550	220,666	282,884	70,547
Composite panels					
Softwood	27,777	22,059	6,448	15,611	5,718
Hardwood	1,610	1,474	646	827	136
Total	29,387	23,533	7,094	16,438	5,854
Poles and posts					
Softwood	9,794	9,396	9,027	369	398
Hardwood	0	0	0	0	0
Total	9,794	9,396	9,027	369	398
Other miscellaneous					
Softwood	512	413	241	172	99
Hardwood	100	88	52	36	12
Total	612	502	294	208	110
Total industrial products					
Softwood	828,095	756,941	508,081	248,860	71,154
Hardwood	273,971	252,822	169,251	83,571	21,149
Total	1,102,066	1,009,763	677,332	332,431	92,303
Domestic fuelwood					
Softwood	2,617	1,190	812	379	1,427
Hardwood	17,069	13,484	11,750	1,735	3,585
Total	19,686	14,675	12,561	2,113	5,011
All products					
Softwood	830,712	758,131	508,892	249,239	72,581
Hardwood	291,040	266,306	181,000	85,306	24,734
Total	1,121,752	1,024,437	689,893	334,544	97,315

Numbers in rows and columns may not sum to totals due to rounding.

Table A.16—Total roundwood output by species group, survey region, and ownership class, Alabama, 2007

Species group and survey region	Total	Ownership class		
		Public	Forest industry	Nonindustrial private
		thousand cubic feet		
Softwoods				
Southwest South	118,586	5,680	26,333	86,573
Southwest North	221,056	6,378	73,835	140,842
Southeast	233,267	5,721	57,462	170,084
West Central	111,222	723	31,896	78,602
North Central	118,623	1,740	23,472	93,411
North	27,958	1,515	0	26,443
Total softwoods	830,712	21,758	212,999	595,955
Hardwoods				
Southwest South	21,375	1,268	2,181	17,926
Southwest North	80,151	6,522	18,357	55,272
Southeast	62,416	54	4,524	57,838
West Central	53,419	743	6,433	46,243
North Central	41,184	3,845	6,374	30,965
North	32,495	1,859	5,312	25,323
Total hardwoods	291,040	14,291	43,181	233,568
All species	1,121,752	36,049	256,180	829,523

Numbers in rows and columns may not sum to totals due to rounding.

Table A.17—Total roundwood output by species group, detailed species group, and product, Alabama, 2007

Species group and detailed species group	Total	Saw logs	Veneer logs	Pulpwood	Composite panels	Poles and posts	Other miscellaneous	Domestic fuelwood
				thousand cubic feet				
Softwood								
Cedar	2,245	874	111	1,170	22	60	1	7
Longleaf-slash pine	93,412	41,569	7,122	41,457	365	2,473	131	295
Loblolly-shortleaf pine	712,739	301,959	51,490	323,839	25,858	6,998	350	2,245
Other yellow pines	21,327	10,103	1,277	8,074	1,532	245	28	67
Cypress	838	401	56	363	0	14	1	3
Hemlock	151	70	13	63	0	4	0	0
Total softwoods	830,712	354,977	60,069	374,966	27,777	9,794	512	2,617
Hardwood								
Soft maple	11,281	2,294	664	7,603	53	0	6	662
Hard maple	868	244	36	534	3	0	0	51
Other birch	1,061	124	34	841	0	0	0	62
Hickory	17,863	3,846	912	11,955	94	0	8	1,048
Beech	2,453	477	107	1,721	4	0	0	144
Ash	2,735	845	208	1,516	6	0	0	160
Black walnut	114	24	3	79	0	0	0	7
Sweetgum	58,520	11,084	3,772	40,012	194	0	26	3,432
Yellow-poplar	29,479	7,273	1,430	18,710	329	0	8	1,729
Blackgum-tupelo	10,419	1,537	396	7,794	78	0	3	611
Sycamore	776	169	9	552	1	0	0	45
Cottonwood	670	238	15	374	4	0	0	39
Black cherry	4,205	850	151	2,934	21	0	2	247
Select white oaks	23,450	6,301	919	14,610	232	0	12	1,375
Other white oaks	14,846	3,614	1,007	9,230	122	0	3	871
Select red oaks	4,917	987	383	3,247	12	0	0	288
Other red oaks	80,430	14,323	3,911	57,140	312	0	28	4,717
Basswood	56	2	7	43	0	0	0	3
Elm	5,020	1,005	324	3,383	13	0	1	295
Other eastern hardwoods	21,878	2,794	812	16,852	132	0	5	1,283
Total hardwoods	291,040	58,030	15,100	199,131	1,610	0	100	17,069
All species	1,121,752	413,007	75,169	574,097	29,387	9,794	612	19,686

Numbers in rows and columns may not sum to totals due to rounding.

Table A.18—Total roundwood output by species group, detailed species group, and ownership class, Alabama, 2007

Species group and detailed species group	Total	Ownership class		
		Public	Forest industry	Nonindustrial private
		thousand cubic feet		
Softwood				
Cedar	2,245	26	473	1,747
Longleaf-slash pine	93,412	4,325	23,652	65,434
Loblolly-shortleaf pine	712,739	16,701	185,718	510,320
Other yellow pines	21,327	656	3,092	17,579
Cypress	838	49	63	725
Hemlock	151	0	0	151
Total softwoods	830,712	21,758	212,999	595,955
Hardwood				
Soft maple	11,281	376	1,584	9,321
Hard maple	868	53	250	565
Other birch	1,061	11	171	879
Hickory	17,863	687	2,872	14,303
Beech	2,453	70	162	2,221
Ash	2,735	119	119	2,497
Black walnut	114	0	1	112
Sweetgum	58,520	2,092	8,614	47,814
Yellow-poplar	29,479	1,038	5,578	22,863
Blackgum-tupelo	10,419	1,281	1,419	7,719
Sycamore	776	219	35	523
Cottonwood	670	0	0	670
Black cherry	4,205	392	701	3,112
Select white oaks	23,450	429	4,298	18,722
Other white oaks	14,845	1,074	2,796	10,975
Select red oaks	4,917	137	794	3,986
Other red oaks	80,430	4,913	10,643	64,874
Basswood	56	0	0	56
Elm	5,020	254	682	4,084
Other eastern hardwoods	21,878	1,146	2,461	18,271
Total hardwoods	291,040	14,291	43,181	233,568
All species	1,121,752	36,049	256,180	829,523

Numbers in rows and columns may not sum to totals due to rounding.